Published by the Arizona Daily Star, a Lee Enterprises Newspaper
Tucson, Arizona 2011

ISBN 978-0-615-51600-4

Cover photo, David Sanders
Book design by Michael Rice

Stories researched by Arizona Daily Star news staff
Photographs taken by Arizona Daily Star photo staff

Tucson Oddities

A COLLECTION OF THE STRANGE SIGHTS THAT MAKE UP THE OLD PUEBLO

Whether it's a piece of art, a historic remnant, an unfinished building or folklore about Tucson, the city has plenty of odd features that pique curiosity.

Beginning in 1999 the Arizona Daily Star published a feature for several years called "What's with that?" which answered readers' questions about different things around Tucson.

In the summer of 2009, the Star brought back the series under the name "Tucson Oddity" as a weekly item. Star readers have submitted hundreds of queries and suggestions.

In 2011, the Star presents readers with Volume I of Tucson Oddities in a book that documents some of the quirky and curious things about the Old Pueblo.

On the cover: The towering neon saguaro stands at the Oracle Road-Main Avenue-Drachman Street interchange. It was lighted for the first time in April 2010.

Arizona Daily Star

TABLE OF CONTENTS

Nowadays, OK Feed & Supply finds itself in the middle of an area known more for home-furnishings stores than dog food and horse feed, but the rooftop horse continues to keep the store identifiable.

Rooftop horse

FIBERGLASS EQUINE ACQUIRED IN 1973 AS PART OF STORE'S PURCHASE

A fiberglass horse that sits atop the roof at OK Feed & Supply often serves as a directional marker for lost motorists trying to navigate the north side of Tucson.

Owner Doug Jordon decided sometime in the 1980s to move the horse from its in-store display because he was running out of room.

More than 20 years later, OK Feed & Supply at 3701 E. Fort Lowell Rd. is as well known for its rooftop equine as it is for its ground-level products, so much so that nearby residents have had trouble coping with its absence at times when the horse was temporarily displaced from its perch.

The red-and-white-painted horse has been stolen at least twice. The most recent theft, in 2001, saw it gone for nearly three weeks before it was found in the middle of the street near East University Boulevard and North Cherry Avenue.

Now the horse — which weighs less than 100 pounds — is bolted not only to the roof, but also to the roof's support beams.

The horse was part of the inventory that Jordon acquired in 1973 when he bought the store from the original owner, O.K. "Bum" Post.

Post, whose given name was Orville Kelvin but was known by everyone as "Bum," opened OK Feed & Supply in 1937 in the heart of the area known then as Binghampton, a Mormon community of farms along the Rillito River.

The lumberjack

SINCE 1964, THE AX-WIELDING BIG GUY HAS STOOD GUARD AT A STRIP MALL

The Paul Bunyan-like statue stands on the corner of Glenn Street and North Stone Avenue in the parking lot of Don's Hot Rod Shop, 2811 N. Stone.

In 1964, the late Leo Toia picked up the 20-foot-tall fiberglass conversation piece while attending a trade show in San Francisco.

Toia, who died in 1988 at the age of 77, first opened a gas station on the property in 1947. He then started carrying auto parts, then seat covers, and eventually moved on to operating a muf-fler shop and a sporting goods store heavy on hunting and fishing equipment.

Today the property houses a number of wide-ranging businesses.

The lumberjack statue has been the target of many vandalism and theft attempts. He's been shot, his ax has been stolen, and once when he was dressed up for Christmas, part of his Santa suit was set on fire.

Even before the big fella was planted into the ground, an attempt was made to pilfer him.

The lumberjack was once dressed up like a member of ZZ Top for a local radio contest, and more recently he was subjected to an unflattering costume for a children's birthday party. He has also worn a tutu.

"There was a homeless guy living in it" when Arizona Exterminating Co. bought the last tower. The company got him an apartment and replaced the cardboard on the windows with glass.

Storm alerts

BEFORE TV, INTERNET, TOWERS ALONG RILLITO MONITORED MONSOON

When the monsoon arrives each summer, Tucson residents can monitor the weather by flipping on the television or logging onto the Internet.

Many years ago, however, farmers living in the area near East Prince and North Country Club roads had to rely on human eyes stationed in watchtowers to spot any potential weather hazards.

Five watchtowers were built along a bend in the nearby Rillito River to help area residents keep watch for powerful monsoon storm.

The last remaining tower is on Arizona Exterminating Co. property at 3149 E. Prince Rd., next to the river.

The grayish tower with a spiral staircase wrapping around the outside was built in the 1950s.

The structure had been unoccupied for about two decades when the exterminating company bought the property 10 years ago.

Now, the three-story tower includes space for pesticides and chemicals, employee records and a workshop.

The skyline of downtown Tucson looms over the businesses of South Sixth Avenue, South Tucson's main drag, much the way the larger city surrounds the smaller one.

Tucson's donut hole

CITY WITHIN THE CITY CAME INTO BEING IN 1936, NEARLY DIDN'T SURVIVE

Incorporated in 1936 as a reaction to fears that annexation by Tucson would lead to higher taxes, the 1.2-square-mile city rests between 40th Street on the south and 26th Street on the north, and between South 12th Avenue on the west and the railroad tracks near South Second Avenue on the east.

South Tucson — with just over 5,500 residents — has its own mayor, Town Council and police and fire departments, although it uses Tucson's utilities and school districts.

The municipality has distinguished itself in both positive and negative ways throughout its history, which started in 1936, when property owners gathered at the Yell-O-Inn auto court to vote the town into existence.

The town nearly evaporated into the ether in 1938 when business owners led a disincorporation campaign to rebel against license-fee increases. Court battles over the disincorporation, as well as Tucson's efforts to annex the town, raged until a March 1939 election reincorporated South Tucson.

In the 1940s, South Tucson elected Iona Stewart as the first female mayor in Arizona.

Its progressiveness was belied by its regressive speed limit, which drew the town a reputation as a speed trap in the 1950s and '60s, when it instituted a 25 mph speed limit in order to generate income.

The city also boasts some of the area's finest Mexican food.

Water tower

SET UP IN 1928 TO SERVE DEVELOPING COLONIA SOLANA NEIGHBORHOOD

The El Conquistador Water Tower at East Broadway and Randolph Way has been listed in the National Register of Historic Places since 1980.

The steel water tower went up in 1928 to serve residents in the then-developing Colonia Solana neighborhood.

The water tower received its first makeover in 1932 when Tucson architect Roy Place hid the tower inside chicken wire and plaster, designed in the Spanish colonial revival style of architecture.

It was restored again in 1994 by the city of Tucson and the Tucson Pima County Historical Commission, with extra assistance from the Arizona Heritage Fund.

The tower is topped by a weather vane depicting a miner and his donkey.

A weather vane depicting a prospector and his donkey sits atop the El Conquistador Water Tower. The tower shares the name but never served the El Conquistador Hotel, which stood where El Con is now.

In addition to the prefabricated gas station, Ralph Montijo built a shed behind the station that he used as an auto shop. "It could hold eight cars," said his son Ralph Jr. "It was a pretty big garage."

Former gas station

LOCATION, GREAT DEPRESSION DOOMED BUSINESS IN ARMORY PARK

The Ralph's Service Station building in historic Armory Park has stood at the corner of South Fourth Avenue and East 19th Street for more than 80 years.

Built around 1929, the station hasn't serviced a vehicle since the late 1930s.

The green-and-white metal building was the first prefabricated gas station in Tucson. It was erected by Ralph Montijo.

The location, along with the Great Depression, brought on the station's demise. Both streets at the intersection were unpaved, and the majority of traffic traveled down Sixth Avenue.

Pat Spoerl of the Oro Valley Historical Society researched the cattle brands by studying a ledger donated to the society, and wrote an essay to educate the community about their meaning.

History marks walls

LIVESTOCK BRANDS ARE PART OF AESTHETICS FOR 2008 ROAD WIDENING

When the Arizona Department of Transportation widened North Oracle Road, or Arizona 77, from Calle Concordia to Pusch View Lane, anti-noise walls and artwork were part of the 2008 project.

Replicas of cattle brands are featured on walls on both sides of Oracle, near the Hilton Tucson El Conquistador Golf & Tennis Resort. They represent ranchers who did business with George Pusch in the early 1900s. Sometime in the 1870s, Pusch, a German immigrant, and Swiss immigrant John Zellweger bought land in what would become Oro Valley and started a cattle ranch.

Part of their ranch is now owned by the town of Oro Valley.

It's known as Steam Pump Ranch.

Once-unwanted art

ONE NEIGHBORHOOD'S TRASH PROVED TO BE ANOTHER ONE'S TREASURE

Public-art pieces "Splash" and "Pipe With Flow 30" sit on the northwest end of Silverlake Park, 1575 E. 36th St.

In 2003, the sculptures were booted from the North Mountain Avenue area, near East Fort Lowell Road, after residents petitioned to get rid of the concrete sculptures, which many could not stomach, calling them ugly.

In 2004, the controversial pieces found a new home after the South Park Neighborhood Association asked the city to put the pieces in the park.

The pieces were created by sculptor Paul Edwards and cost the city $83,000. It cost about $6,000 to remove the artwork.

"Pipe With Flow 30" was supposed to show stormwater flowing between two drainage pipes, and "Splash" was meant to show water gushing out of upright pipes.

Bike church

FRAMES, WHEELS MAKE UP THIS MEMORIAL FOR CYCLISTS KILLED ON ROADS

The Bike Church on Granada Avenue near Barrio Anita is a walk-in metal sculpture made of bike parts, stained-glass windows and musical chimes.

The sculpture's stained-glass windows resemble those of a church; the top is similar to those on Islamic temples; and there are two Stars of David on the sides and a mold of a Pascua Yaqui dancer, said Joseph O'Connell, one of the artists behind the Bike Church.

It serves as a permanent memorial for cyclists killed on the streets.

The hundreds of bike frames, wheels and rims make up the white high-ceilinged structure that sits on city-owned land at the southwest corner of North Granada Avenue and West Davis Street, near West St. Mary's Road.

The 22-foot-tall sculpture is illuminated with solar power.

O'Connell and Blessing Hancock of Creative Machines created the sculpture with the help of eight students in 2009. The Ward 1 City Council office, with a $50,000 grant from the Pima Association of Governments and support from cyclists in the region, employed the students for eight weeks to work on the project.

The Bike Church was completed on Aug. 14, 2009.

Artists assisted by eight students and a grant from the Pima Association of Governments completed the Bike Church in August 2009.

Gila-monster sculptures rest on the median where West Irvington Road crosses the Santa Cruz River's West Branch near South Mission Road.

Gila monsters

RECYCLED PRODUCTS HELPED 2 SCULPTURES COME TO LIFE IN 1993

Commuters on Irvington Road west of the Santa Cruz River are treated to the sight of two gigantic tile-covered Gila monster sculptures.

Resting on the median on West Irvington Road just east of South Mission Road, the twin 52-foot-long Gilas were designed and built in 1993 by a team led by local architect Bob Vint.

The Gila monsters were built up on internal frames, sprayed with the concrete mixture Gu-nite and covered with inlaid fragments of colored tiles, ceramics, porcelain, mirrors and other objects, such as spark plugs, horseshoes, pool balls, toy cars, cowrie shells and teacup handles.

The ceramic tiles were reject pieces donated by the Mexican Tile Co.

The project cost about $75,000 to build and took close to six months to complete.

"That truck is still sitting on the same building I originally put it on," said Spencer Brown, who owns the shed company. "If customers are looking for us, we just say that we're the guys with the truck."

Shed-top truck

OLD CHEVY WAS MEANT TO DEMONSTRATE HOW TOUGH FIRM'S SHEDS WERE

There's a shed-sitting truck at the headquarters of The Original Shed and Garage Co., 3424 S. Campbell Ave.

It was placed there in the mid-1990s to emphasize the sturdy structure of the sheds.

The company was formerly known as Tuff Shed. Workers used a crane to hoist the old Chevrolet truck to its new home more than 8 feet off the ground.

It's been going nowhere fast ever since.

Pancho Villa

BRONZE STATUE OF MEXICAN REVOLUTIONARY LOOMS LARGE DOWNTOWN

A bronze statue of Pancho Villa can be found at Veinte de Agosto Park, between West Broadway and West Congress Street downtown.

Villa was a general in the Mexican Revolution and was assassinated in 1923. Some revere him as a hero who liberated the poor and disenfranchised, while others dismiss him as a thief and murderer of innocents.

American soldiers pursued Villa after he and his rebels killed 18 Americans in Columbus, N.M., on March 9, 1916. The attack was in retaliation against the American government, which Villa claimed was supporting an enemy regime.

Spanish-born sculptor Julian Martinez and foundry man Javier Portilla created the statue, which was given to the state of Arizona on June 30, 1981. The statue — which is 14 feet tall and weighs 7 tons — survived two lawsuits that attempted to stop it from being erected. The Villa sculpture came to Tucson only after the Phoenix-area town of Guadalupe rejected it.

Then-Mayor Lew Murphy refused to attend the dedication, which was attended by 1,000 supporters.

The man known as El Centauro del Norte, the centaur of the north, sits appropriately on horseback in Veinte de Agosto Park in downtown Tucson. He's been there since the early 1980s.

The Pima Trails Association, a local equestrian group, got the idea for the buttons after seeing something similar in California horse country.

Tall pedestrians?

BUTTONS LET RIDERS STAY IN THE SADDLE WHILE WAITING TO CROSS ROAD

There are two sets of pedestrian push buttons on some Foothills corners.

The higher of the two silver buttons, about 6 feet off the ground, isn't meant to accommodate an abundance of overly tall people in the area.

Rather it's to make it easier for people on horseback to safely cross busy intersections in parts of town where equestrian life still exists.

The double buttons can be found at four intersections: East River Road and North Alvernon Way, River and North Pontatoc Road, Alvernon and North Dodge Boulevard, and North Cray-croft Road and East Territory Drive.

All of those intersections were upgraded as part of road-widening projects done by Pima County.

Plans for the widening of North La Cañada Drive call for similar equestrian buttons where La Cañada crosses West Orange Grove, West Ina and West Magee roads, Pima County Department of Transportation officials said.

Though at other places equestrians can dismount to press crossing buttons, having them higher up makes things safer for riders.

The late Jerry Hall filled his yard near East Grant Road and North Campbell Avenue with the odd little critters. After his death, his widow decided to keep them in the yard.

Chrome characters

LATE ARTIST CONSTRUCTED MANY WHILE GOING THROUGH CHEMOTHERAPY

This home in central Tucson attracts many drive-up visitors who admire the chrome and metal sculptures that adorn the yard.

Created by the late Jerry Hall, the collection includes robotic figures; musicians jamming on a guitar, banjo and trumpet; and an army of warriors. The sculptures have been video-taped and photographed by University of Arizona art students and by motorists who frequently stop to take in the show.

Jerry and his sculptures were shown on the Discovery Channel's "Offbeat America," and they also were featured in "Weird Arizona" by Wesley Treat.

Some of the sculptures were created by Jerry when he was going through chemotherapy. His widow plans to keep them in family yard at 1402 E. Water St., at the corner of North Highland Avenue. The neighborhood is north of East Grant Road and west of North Campbell Avenue.

Watchful woman

METAL MISS RECALLS RESTAURANT THAT CLOSED 20-PLUS YEARS AGO

A copper-colored woman with protruding eyelashes made of rebar stands against a building on East Grant Road near North Country Club Road.

The sculpture is one of the last remnants of the former Tia Elena restaurant, which occupied the building more than 20 years ago. Sculptor Jesus C. Corral founded the restaurant in the 1960s, but it's unknown if he created the copper-colored woman.

The sculpture served as a chimney for the restaurant.

The sculpture's eyes and earrings were illuminated, although currently no light bulbs are in the sockets. A later owner planned to build a fence around the sculpture to protect it from vandals.

Did the star of "Gone With the Wind," "It Happened One Night" and "Soldier of Fortune" live in this house? Neighborhood legend says yes, but no one can say for sure.

Clark Gable's place?

IT'S UNCLEAR IF THE FILM STAR LIVED THERE, BUT HE DID SPEND TIME HERE

There's a large house near East Grant Road and North Alvernon Way with a sign labeling it "The Gable House." Neighborhood legend has it Clark Gable lived there for a year as he mourned the death of his wife, Carole Lombard, who died in the crash of TWA Flight 3 in January 1942.

Many dispute that he lived there, but Gable did like to spend time in the Old Pueblo.

According to a Jan. 2, 1948, Star interview with Gable at the Arizona Inn, where he often retreated between films:

"Just before the death of his wife, Carole Lombard, stunned the nation, Gable and she were in Tucson shopping for a ranch. He said, however, that he has lost interest in living on a big ranch since that fatal plane crash," the article said.

City golf officials never considered tearing down the barn during renovations at the course in 2005. "It's still something different out there in the middle of a golf course," one said.

Golf course adobe

WHAT'S LEFT OF BARN SITS AT FIFTH TEE OF SILVERBELL GOLF COURSE

The adobe structure which sits near the fifth tee box at Silverbell Golf Course isn't so much of an obstacle as it is a curiosity.

The structure is an adobe barn with four crumbling walls and no roof. It's what's left of an old cotton farm.

The course, on Silverbell Road north of Ironwood Hill Drive, is operated by the city and was dedicated in 1979. In 2005 it was renovated because part of the course was built on a city landfill and the greens were sinking.

City of Tucson officials preserved the barn during renovations because its presence is interesting.

The structure doesn't meet requirements to be designated a historical landmark.

Movie prop

OLD DRILL PRESS CAME BACK HOME AFTER FILM CREW WAS DONE WITH IT

A prop from the movie "The Postman" sits at the corner of East Grant Road and North Seventh Avenue.

Kent Solberg, co-owner of Kent's Tools, sold the drill press to the movie production company and then bought the piece of machinery back when it no longer was needed for filming.

The 1997 movie, with Kevin Costner starring in a story about post-apocalyptic America, was partly filmed in the Tucson area.

Kent's Tools manager Larry Duncan said he's tried unsuccessfully to spot the drill press in the movie. "I looked for it a couple of times, but I've never seen it," he said.

The drill press could be anywhere from 75 to 100 years old.

Kent Solberg has sold or rented other pieces of equipment used as props in films, including the 1995 movie "Tank Girl." "We'd sell them to movie sets and buy them back if they were in reasonable shape."

PAGE 33

Desert lighthouse

ROTATING BEAM OF LIGHT MARKS FORMER HOME OF RELIGIOUS GROUPS

Standing about 15 feet tall, the lighthouse south of Tucson lights up at night and blinks a rotating ray of light.

It sits on 3.8 acres at 10080 S. Nogales High-way, along with a house of worship that has been home to at least two congregations.

The lighthouse was constructed in 1990.

There are no ships to warn of shoals, but a lighthouse sits nonetheless on South Nogales Highway a little southwest of Tucson International Airport.

Road to nowhere

2-MILE STRETCH BESIDE I-10 LEADS TO NOTHING, THEN JUST DEAD-ENDS

Most roads lead to something, but not this one.

The two-mile stretch of worn, weathered, weed-lined highway leads to no houses, no businesses, no farm fields — nothing. And then it comes to a dead end.

It's at Exit 279 on Interstate 10 southeast of Tucson on the frontage road immediately north of I-10, paralleling the freeway.

The Arizona Department of Transportation says the road section was part of a highway that predated I-10.

It remains open for access to utilities and outdoor advertising.

To find this oddity, take the Colossal Cave Road exit off Interstate 10. The segment running to the northwest, paralleling the freeway, is a road with no apparent reason.

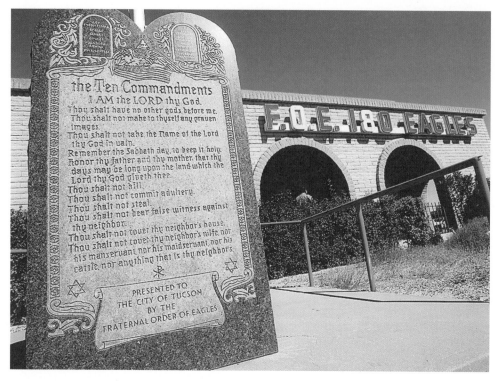

"The Ten Commandments," a 1956 movie starring Charlton Heston as Moses, was the inspiration for national officials of the Fraternal Order of Eagles to give local lodges the stone tablets.

Heed the stone

COMMANDMENTS CARVED IN GRANITE PLANTED OUTSIDE EAGLES LODGE

A large granite tablet of the Ten Commandments catches the eyes of motorists passing by the Fraternal Order of Eagles Aerie 180 at 1530 N. Stone Ave.

The gray-and-black granite monolith is about 6 feet tall and 3 feet wide.

It was presented by the national order in the 1960s.

The national order dedicated the monoliths to cities and public institutions after the release of the movie "The Ten Commandments" starring Charlton Heston, Yul Brynner and Anne Baxter.

"The cactus almost certainly does not graft to the host plant, but its roots simply cling to the surfaces and gather rainfall," said Mark Dimmitt, director of natural history at the Arizona-Sonora Desert Museum.

Prickly situation

FREE-SPIRITED CACTUS FINDS AN UNUSUAL HOME IN CATALINA STATE PARK

Cacti have a long and quite successful history of growing out of the ground.

Sinking roots into dirt just seems to work.

Now and then, though, a free-spirited cactus takes a very different approach.

One example: a prickly pear cactus growing out of the trunk of a mesquite tree in Catalina State Park north of Tucson.

It is visible along a stretch of the short Canyon Loop Trail in the park.

Those in the know say cactus roots can absorb large amounts of water and survive for many months without rain.

Splashing memories

TOWER WAS AN INDOOR STAIRCASE FOR THREE ENCLOSED WATER SLIDES

The barren brick tower that juts out at the top, near Interstate 10 and Ina Road is remembered by longtime Tucsonans as the indoor staircase that led to three enclosed water slides at the former Sportspark.

The 1,100 feet of tubing can now be found at Marana's Breakers Water Park, but the tower remains at the Ina facility, now called Mike Jacob Sports Park.

The tubes were moved to Breakers in 1996.

Pima County, which owns the tower, plans to demolish the obsolete tower at some point.

The tower hides only an indoor staircase that now leads nowhere, but longtime Tucsonans remember it as home to a cooling ride down a tube full of water on many a hot summer day.

"I'm an electrical contractor, but I had done a lot of yard art, and this seemed like the right memorial for Brian," Larry Wilson said. "I used parts from his truck."

Roadside robot

SCULPTURE SERVES AS MEMORIAL TO MOTORCYCLE ACCIDENT VICTIM

A little figure labeled "Brian" sits along 22nd Street, across from Palo Verde High School.

It is a memorial to 24-year-old Brian Wilson, an expert auto mechanic who died in a motorcycle accident Dec. 20, 2008.

The robot-like figure was made of car parts by Brian's father, Larry Wilson, with help from family members. It stands at the accident site in the 6800 block of East 22nd Street.

A truck's sound-system speaker serves as the figure's head. A muffler forms the torso; springs stand in for legs; and shock absorbers represent the arms.

The name "Brian" on the front of the figure was etched onto a piece of metal by Brian himself a year or so before the accident.

The public-art project is joined in Sentinel Plaza, at West Congress Street and I-10, by a smaller monolith decorated in tile and the "spirit" line that zigzags across the plaza's floor.

Monoliths

RAMMED-EARTH SCULPTURE A REMINDER OF ANCIENT TUCSONANS' HOMES

Four rammed-earth monoliths stand at the northwest corner of West Congress Street and Interstate 10, in Sentinel Plaza.

The hard-to-miss sculptures — the tallest monolith is 28 feet tall — went up in late 2001, but the surrounding plaza, which is named after Sentinel Peak or "A" Mountain, wasn't completed until 2003.

The monoliths face "A" Mountain and are intended to offer a connection to the city's ancient inhabitants, who lived along the Santa Cruz River and built their dwellings out of the earth.

The site at one time was home to the Desert Inn, but the hotel was demolished to make way for wider I-10 frontage roads.

A group of artists that included Joy Fox, Andrew Rush, Chuck Sternberg, Judith Stewart and architect Bob Vint designed the public art project.

The monoliths and the surrounding plaza were built with two $250,000 federal grants awarded to the Arizona Department of Transportation.

LUCKY WISHBONE

DELICIOUS
CHICKEN

SHRIMP

Flashing sign

NEON STAR INCORPORATED INTO LUCKY WISHBONE'S LOGO

The flashing, neon star with the strobe-like burst of white light stands in front of the Lucky Wishbone on North Swan Road near Broadway.

The sign, whose iconic image is incorporated into the company's logo for its six locations in Tucson, was designed and erected in 1953 by Arizona Neon.

Because the sign was "grandfathered" by the city, property owners can't replace the bulb on the south side of the sign, which is why it flashes only on the north face.

Fans of the "Bone" are rabid, judging from its Facebook page, where patrons pine for their steak fingers and fried gizzards from as far away as the Congo.

The price tag — $88,000 — and general concerns about its appearance made Washington, D.C., artist Athena Tacha's work controversial at first. But over three decades, it grew on us.

Clothespin art

SCULPTURE AT EAST END OF UA MALL HAS BECOME A SYMBOL OF SCHOOL

The University of Arizona's trademark set of 16-foot-high wishbones, a sculpture titled "Curving Arcades: Homage to Bernini," was completed in 1981.

The sculpture is by Athena Tacha, a Washington, D.C.-based public artist. It was commissioned by the UA Museum of Art and was initial-ly met with grumbling both over its price — about $88,000 — and appearance.

Student leaders wanted to rip it out.

But years of "Curving Arcades" showing up in promotional brochures and visitors' guides have made the sculpture emblematic of the UA.

"The mountains are seen as holy places to the Tohono O'odham," said Martín Rivera, a former manager of the Mission Branch Library.

Mountain monoliths

SEVENTEEN STONE WALLS IN FORMATION NEAR MISSION BRANCH LIBRARY

Seventeen monoliths can be found at the northwest corner of West Ajo Way and South Mission Road, near the Mission Branch Library.

The stone walls are known as Many Color Mountain, or Na: nko Ma: s Du'ag Son in the language of the Tohono O'odham tribe near Tucson.

The impressions of children's handprints are on the backs of the towers.

The public art was done by Chris Tanz, Susan Holman and the late Paul T. Edwards. It was dedicated in December 1994 and cost the city's Transportation Department $55,950.

Tail-wing art

SCULPTURE FROM SALVAGED PLANE PART GRACES THE FRONT OF GALLERY

The 18-foot-tall sculpture crafted from the tail wing of a C-130 cargo plane is made of aluminum, concrete, steel and wood, with a lighted doorway built into the base.

The wing sculpture was part of a collection of pieces made from airplane parts salvaged from the Aerospace Maintenance and Regeneration Center, better known as the Boneyard, at Davis-Monthan Air Force Base.

It has sat in front of Dabney and Tom Philabaum's gallery and studio on South Sixth Avenue near downtown Tucson for years.

Gallery owner Tom Philabaum figured an airport- or aviation-themed museum would have shown interest in buying the sculpture by now. But after 20 years, no takers.

Gargoyles and more

STATUES SERVE A FENG SHUI PURPOSE AT HOME-BASED BUSINESS

Gargoyles, angels and cherubs line the roof of the home of Eric Cuestas-Thompson and Michael Bamba.

The 50 statues, painted gold, copper and bronze, resemble sentinels on watch in a quiet neighborhood just south of East Speedway and east of North Alvernon Way. They serve a feng shui purpose.

Feng shui — a Chinese philosophy dating back 7,000 years — links design and space arrangement to a flow of energy. It's aimed at achieving harmony and balance in one's environment and in one's life, proponents say.

The philosophy led Bamba and Cuestas-Thompson to open their business, Those Feng Shui Guys. They operate the business at their home at 940 N. Longfellow Ave. Cuestas-Thompson also runs a psychotherapy practice from a building on the property.

The partners began Those Feng Shui Guys in 2006 after graduating from the Western School of Feng Shui in Encinitas, Calif. Their clients include businesses and homeowners.

Each image and setting is there for a purpose, explained Eric Cuestas-Thompson, who added that there is "positive energy released from each arrangement."

Colorful bull

HE SUFFERS ALL MANNER OF INDIGNITIES OUTSIDE EAST-SIDE RESTAURANT

The bull and matador in front of Casa Molina is a symbol of restaurant owner Gilberto L. Molina's fondness for bullfighting and ranching.

And the bull's multicolored testicles?

Those are the object of scavenger hunts, photos and the curiosity of passers-by.

The statue has been in front of the family restaurant at 6226 E. Speedway since the early 1960s.

The sculpture was created by Lee Koplin.

As for the testicles, the restaurant does not paint the body parts. Numerous groups, ranging from fraternities and sororities to car clubs, have shown up with spray cans to colorize the bull's genitalia.

The matador has been fighting the bull outside Casa Molina, on East Speedway near North Wilmot Road, since the early 1960s.

It's an Allstate Insurance office today, but for nearly 60 years the art deco structure with the swirl on top served as a gas station. It even appeared in a movie.

Soft-serve building

OLD GAS STATION NOW AN INSURANCE OFFICE — SORRY, BUT NO CONES

With a roof that resembles a soft-serve ice cream cone, the building at 648 N. Stone Ave. — near Fourth Street — was once a service station.

It was built in 1924 and known as Old Pueblo Station for decades. The art deco structure might have been used to advertise goodies to those who wanted to fill their bellies along with their gas tanks.

In 1973 it became a Union 76 station and can be viewed in a scene in the 1980 movie "Stir Crazy." The station closed in 1981.

Today, the building's owner operates an insurance and accounting firm there.

Artist Jake Honeycutt always thought the sculpture was a boy, "so I called it Fred, or Bob from time to time," but its new owner says it's a girl. "So I guess it's whatever people want it to be."

The lizard-fish

ANIMAL-COMBINATION SCULPTURE HAS SADDLES FOR POTENTIAL 'RIDERS'

The 12-foot-long sculpture sits on the sidewalk on South Third Avenue just north of East 20th Street, across the street from Santa Rita Park. It was designed and constructed by local artist Jake Honeycutt about six years ago.

Honeycutt began the design process with just the shape — he wanted to make something that curved around like a wave.

Once the sculpture took on the shape of a fish, Honeycutt needed a way to make the steel and concrete piece stay in place. That's when the lizard legs came in.

Honeycutt then painted blue scales and armorlike details on the colorful sculpture, turning it into a big medieval lizard-fish. He also put two saddles on it for kids, or adults, to sit on and enjoy.

Honeycutt initially planned to give the sculpture to the Tucson Children's Museum, but representatives had concerns about children riding it and considered it playground material, not a sculpture.

Post-9/11 tribute

ANGEL ON SOUTH-SIDE CORNER SYMBOLIZES RISING FROM THE RUBBLE

On the southwest corner of East Irvington Road and South Tucson Boulevard sits an angel sculpture built in the summer of 2002 by high school students under the direction of local artist David Campbell.

Campbell and eight students created the angel sculpture, which is painted an eye-catching blue, as part of a youth-enrichment project with ties to the Tucson Pima Arts Council.

Resting on the angel is a slab that reads: "Together We Rise."

The artists wanted their sculpture to have meaning, Campbell said.

"It was looking at a post-9/11 world," he said. "That's why it says 'Together We Rise.' It's rising above the rubble."

"Together We Rise," on the main road to Tucson International Airport, dates to the summer of 2002. It emphasizes hope after the devastation of the Sept. 11, 2001, terror attacks.

Boulders don't last long outside when UA students in mining engineering get after them. After a few years of drilling competitions, they have to be replaced.

Holey boulder

POCKMARKS STEM FROM UA'S ENGINEERS' WEEK DRILLING COMPETITIONS

A large boulder graces the east side of Old Main on the University of Arizona campus — but it's not exactly in its natural state. The rock is painted with a black grid pattern and pock-marked with more than three dozen holes.

The neat, cylindrical holes were created during drilling competitions by students enrolled in the UA Department of Mining and Geological Engineering.

Participants in the competitions — usually held during Engineers' Week in February — use powerful drills to bore holes in large boulders placed near Old Main.

Rocks used for the drilling competitions eventually become so full of holes that they need to be replaced.

The Central Arizona Project's "one size fits all" no-trespassing sign usually lands along canals or other water features, but it's pretty much out of place near Pima Community College's Desert Vista Campus.

No kidding

NO SWIMMING? NO FISHING? NO PROBLEM, BECAUSE THERE'S NO WATER

A metal sign from the Central Arizona Project hanging on a barbed-wire fence that borders the east side of the street makes it clear: "NO TRES-PASSING, NO FISHING, NO SWIMMING."

And, to drive the point home, there are illus-trations.

But the dusty plot of fenced-in desert land north of Valencia Road just west of Interstate 19 is totally dry.

Turns out the Central Arizona Project, which owns the land, only has one type of "No Tres-

passing" sign for all of its properties along the 336-mile canal it administers. The CAP stretches from Lake Havasu City to south of Tucson. The canal delivers Colorado River water to Central and Southern Arizona.

The fence is guarding a set of incomplete pow-er lines from a nearby substation that the CAP is planning to eventually connect to its power grid.

Swimming and fishing in the canal are prohib-ited for safety reasons. The entire length of the canal is fenced.

Sand trout

ARCHITECT, ARTIST UNITE TO PRESENT MYTHICAL RIVER CREATURES

The Santa Cruz sand trout is the local version of a unicorn, a mythical creature whose legend has been passed down through generations.

"Endemic to the dry washes of Southern Arizona, this fish is able to withstand extreme heat and the absence of water," claims a plaque affixed to a bridge on East Tanque Verde Road near North Pima Street, where a pair of metal sculptures rising from the Rose Hill Wash honor the sand trout.

Local architect Paul Edwards and local artist Chris Tanz designed the sculptures —which rotate when windy — for $25,000 in 1997 as part of a city-funded public-art piece.

As the story goes, the sand trout first lived in the Santa Cruz River back when it still flowed. Once it ran dry, the sand trout developed the ability to breathe air and live in the sand.

Tucson folklorist Jim Griffith's 1988 book "Southern Arizona Folk Arts" notes that sand trout is quite a delicacy. That is, if you can manage to bag one.

Farmer John mural

IT ADORNS WALL AROUND FORMER MEATPACKING PLANT AT GRANT, I-10

The Farmer John Meats building's wall mural remains a well-known sight to Tucson motorists.

Painted in 1963 by Leslie Grimes, a former Hollywood scene painter, the panoramic mural depicts dozens of cattle charging through the desert on an outer wall along the building at West Grant Road and Interstate 10.

Farmer John's parent, Clougherty Packing Co., closed the facility in August 2001.

The building got a new tenant in 2010 — at least for the month of October, when a local haunted-house operator moved in and began converting it into "The Slaughter House."

The herd stampedes silently on, and its building has been envisioned as the site for many a new venture, including a country-Western bar. It was turned into The Slaughter House for Halloween.

Tick tock

PEDESTAL CLOCK IN DOWNTOWN PARK WAS NEARLY SIGN-CODE VICTIM

A 16-foot-high pedestal topped by a massive clock sits along the west side of Church Avenue between Congress Street and Broadway.

The timepiece is often referred to as the Daniel's Jewelers clock because of the name emblazoned on the clock's face.

It was moved there in the 1980s after city employees fought the Tucson City Council's attempts to get the clock taken down because it violated the city's new sign codes.

More than $18,000 was spent at the time by Gordon Jewelers to have the clock refurbished and planted in concrete on the eastern edge of Veinte de Agosto Park.

Gordon had owned the clock since 1962, when original owner Elmer Present — who opened Daniel's Jewelers downtown in 1926 — sold his store to Gordon.

City employees fought an attempt by the City Council to have the clock removed, and after $18,000 in restoration work it was placed in Veinte de Agosto Park.

The tower originally was designed as a fountain in the mid-1960s. It stands at the corner of Via Entrada and East River Road.

A fountain no more

MODERNISTIC TOWER ONCE FLOWED, NOW STANDS AS DISTINCTIVE LANDMARK

Developers of a master-planned community in the Foothills sought to make the entrance to one neighborhood stand out by installing a large stone tower that would double as a fountain.

The tower, which stands on the north side of the intersection of East River Road and North Via Entrada, was commissioned in 1966 by John W. Murphey and was designed by Mexican architect Juan Warner Baz. Baz was looking for something different for Neighborhood No. 7 — the first in Pima County to use a pod-style development layout.

The tower was to have water fill the hollow interior, flow off the top of each of the tiers of block and then cascade down the sides.

Unfortunately, when the wind blew, the spray from the fountain was soaking cars, and the water feature was disconnected.

"I just wanted something whimsical," said artist Joe Tyler. "I wanted something that would put a smile on people's faces when they walk or drive by."

Lounging lizards

WELDED STEEL CREATURES BASK IN THE SUN AS RESULT OF ROAD PROJECT

Fanciful lizards made of welded steel are perched on boulders in front of a row of shops and businesses near East Pima Street and North Craycroft Road.

Artist Joe Tyler created them as public art as part of the road-improvement project on Pima Street.

Some of the lizards appear to be watching traffic. Others look to be just lazing. And one clings to the side of a rock near a bus stop.

Empty message

BIG CIRCLE IN SKY NEXT TO I-10 LIVES ON LONG AFTER GAS STATION LEFT

The vacant commercial property along Interstate 10 comes complete with its own 100-foot-tall circular sign that can be seen for blocks.

The northwest corner of East Benson Highway and South Park Avenue sits vacant, except for the sign that used to represent the Union 76 gas station that opened there in the mid-1950s.

Look closely at the sign and you still can see the outline of the "76" on both sides of the circle, which has been painted white to cover the logo's orange-and-blue color scheme.

The sign still has light bulbs in the fixtures that hang over where gas prices were displayed.

Why is the sign still there? Chalk it up to Tucson's sign ordinances, which allow signs of that size to exist only if they predate the establishment of the code in 1985, said its property agent.

"I get phone calls every once in a while from people asking if they can buy them," owner Michael Coretz said. "I tell them it would cost more to move them with a crane than what they're offering to pay."

London calling

3 CAST-IRON BRITISH PHONE BOOTHS WEIGH IN AT 1,700 POUNDS EACH

Three cast-iron phone booths decorate the Casa del Arroyo apartment complex at North Norris Avenue and East Seventh Street. They were imported from London about 20 years ago by complex owner Michael Coretz, a real estate broker for Commercial Real Estate Group.

His brother, Craig, bought the booths in London from British Telecom in 1990. Each booth cost $90, plus $210 for delivery. Craig Coretz, who lived in Chicago and died in 2009, bought several of the booths, sold them for scrap metal and gave the three remaining booths to Michael.

The booths weigh 1,700 pounds. They were appraised at between $1,800 and $2,000 20 years ago.

TEP sold the land, and what's left of the building, to Arizona Plumbing Supply, according to Pima County Assessor's Office records. "I've been looking after it for a number of years," said owner David Campbell.

Substation shell

IT'S ALL THAT REMAINS OF FORMER TEP INSTALLATION AT STONE, PRINCE

A brick-and-mortar shell of a building on the northwest corner of North Stone Avenue and West Prince Road elicits much curiosity. That building is what is left of a Tucson Electric Power substation.

TEP stopped using the substation in the 1990s when other substations were built as TEP's coverage expanded.

The property was subsequently sold.

Stylish mannequin

FASHIONABLE DILLARD'S REFUGEE ADORNS DOWNTOWN-AREA BALCONY

She dresses for any occasion, changes her hairdo often and can be spotted with hats and crowns.

Owner Carmen Martinez Mandros bought the mannequin from Dillard's in the late 1990s when the department store was readying to move from El Con Mall to Park Mall.

She was named Athena — after the Greek goddess of wisdom, justice and war — and sits on the second-story balcony of the Mandros home on South Scott Avenue, near the Temple of Music and Art.

Mandros got the idea after a visit to Paris, where she saw an apartment balcony with several mannequins dressed as though they were attending a party.

The mannequin's name is Athena, but local businesswoman Dorothy Kret, a big fan, calls her Miss M. "This is so totally Tucson." she says. "Where else would someone do this?"

In its day, which dates to the 1920s, the odd little structure on the north side of the Stone Avenue underpass has supplied fuel for both people and their automobiles.

Busy building

IT WAS RESTAURANT, THEN A CAFE/GAS STATION, THEN JUST A GAS STOP

This structure was originally built around 1923, when construction began on the Stone Avenue underpass. The first mention of 503 N. Stone Ave. in the old Tucson city directories that were published annually was in 1928, when it was listed as an unnamed restaurant owned by M.L. Stephenson.

By 1930, the property had morphed into a combination cafe and gas station.

A picture of the corner, showing an "independent" gas station selling Dixie gas and a restaurant called Earl's Place, was included in the 1985 book "From Main Street to Miracle Mile," by Demion Clinco of the Tucson Historic Preservation Foundation.

From 1931 to 1947, city directories listed Southland Oil Co. as the property owner.

By 1948, the property was known as the Schumann Service Station, according to city directories, and T.W. Schumann remained the listed owner until the property was sold in 1957 to longtime Tucsonan Patrick Tanno.

If you've ever craved the natural-world equivalent of a "perp walk" or jail-yard ramble, this could be the perfect place for you.

Trail of no deviation

FENCED-IN FOOTHILLS STRETCH KEEPS HIKERS OFF ADJACENT PRIVATE LAND

A trail hemmed in on both sides with 8-foot-high chain-link fences topped with barbed wire can be found on Tucson's north side. The half-mile trail, with a county-maintained trailhead at the northern end of Campbell Avenue, may project a certain aura of incarceration — but it also has a practical purpose.

The route serves as a public easement through private residential property to nation-al forest lands.

The fences and barbed wire are intended to keep hikers on the trail and off private land.

The fenced route was installed when the area was developed in the late 1980s to provide passage to a popular rock-climbing site known as Campbell Cliff.

The cliff, which is on private land, is now off-limits to the public.

Spiky lights

LOOK CLOSELY, USE YOUR IMAGINATION AND MAYBE YOU'LL SEE PALM TREES

The structure at the Wilmot Road entrance of Park Place, 5870 E. Broadway, is artwork, placed there during the mall's renovation in 2000.

It was placed there to go with the mall's theme of palm trees.

The structure is topped with light bulbs that are automatically activated at night and stay on for one hour after the last movie ends at the Century 20 theater.

A similar structure greets visitors at the mall's entrance on Chantilly Drive off of Broadway. The one on Wilmot is more elaborate and has more lights.

"I know they've been trying to make the mall look 'deserty,' " said an employee at a store in Park Place. "It kind of looks like a Picasso version of a palm tree."

Hillside shrine

FORMER INMATE PUT IT THERE IN THANKS FOR RELEASE FROM COUNTY JAIL

On Father's Day in 1993, Pancho Murrietta put a statue of Our Lady of Guadalupe in a grotto on the side of "A" Mountain off South Mission Road. He wanted to give thanks for his release from the Pima County jail, where he had been locked up for a crime he says he did not commit.

People walk up to the shrine and pray, and it has grown to include other religious items and candles.

Over the years, vandals have smashed the religious statues and candles left there by people who make pilgrimages to the shrine. Others quickly replace damaged items.

Before his death in 2006, Bishop Manuel D. Moreno of the Roman Catholic Diocese of Tucson hoped to construct a chapel at the base of the mountain. Five years later, the project has yet to be completed.

Pancho Murrietta's shrine to Our Lady of Guadalupe is on "A" Mountain, not that far from the Pima County jail, where Murrietta was held on a crime he says he didn't commit.

Giant wine bottle

IT WAS ONCE PART OF ITALIAN RESTAURANT'S MOTIF BEFORE BOONDOCKS

The Boondocks Lounge is hard to miss with its 35-foot-tall wine bottle standing out front.

The roadside attraction — a purple-and-green-painted Chianti bottle — is at 3306 N. First Ave.

The Boondocks' bottle has a real cork top and a back door, which is not padlocked shut, that once served as entry to storage space.

The Chianti bottle arrived at the site in 1974 as part of the design for an Italian restaurant known as the Peasant Villa. Original owners William H. and Georgann Muniz commissioned noted artist Michael Kautza to build the concrete-and-rebar bottle for $3,500.

Artist Michael Kautza, who built the bottle, also made the Tack Room's famous boot as well as the giant cow skull, visible from Interstate 19, at the Cow Palace in Amado.